TREES

By Emilie Dufresne

Minneapolis, Minnesota

Credits:
Front Cover – Maria Symchych, WARUT PINAMKA, 4&5 – oliveromg, sirtravelalot, 6&7 – VP Photo Studio, narikan, 8&9 – Sergey Novikov, gorillaimages, 10&11 – Oksana Mizina, Aleksei Potov, Lynn Yeh, 12&13 – suefeldberg/iStock, nnattalli, Mukhanova/iStock, domnicky/iStock, 14&15 – Suphaya Wachiraboworntham/iStock, franconiaphoto, Nataly Studio, Vastram, mama_mia, 16&17 – novodka, Eye Visual, Arts, AlessandraRC, Zakharova_Natalia/iStock, 18&19 – Ania Saenz de Urturi, O de R, Diyana Dimitrova, erperlstrom/iStock, 20&21 – Zaitsava Olga, EvgeniiAnd, Deniza 40x, 22&23 – kornnphoto, MintImages. Images are courtesy of Shutterstock.com. With thanks to Getty Images, Thinkstock Photo, and iStockphoto.

Library of Congress Cataloging-in-Publication Data is available at www.loc.gov or upon request from the publisher.

ISBN: 978-1-63691-466-4 (hardcover)
ISBN: 978-1-63691-473-2 (paperback)
ISBN: 978-1-63691-480-0 (ebook)

© 2022 Booklife Publishing
This edition is published by arrangement with Booklife Publishing.

North American adaptations © 2022 Bearport Publishing Company. All rights reserved. No part of this publication may be reproduced in whole or in part, stored in any retrieval system, or transmitted in any form or by any means, electronic, mechanical, photocopying, recording, or otherwise, without written permission from the publisher.

For more information, write to Bearport Publishing, 5357 Penn Avenue South, Minneapolis, MN 55419. Printed in the United States of America.

CONTENTS

Welcome to the Forest 4

Taking Care of Nature 6

Into the Woods 8

Busy Bark..................... 10

Sticks and Seeds............... 12

Fruit and Nuts................. 14

Changing Colors 16

New Growth 18

Get Making!................... 20

Time to Think.................. 22

Glossary 24

Index 24

WELCOME TO THE FOREST

Welcome to forest school. Let's explore, play, and create!

Get ready for forest fun!

We can learn so much from the world around us. Step outside into a great big classroom full of trees.

What do you want to learn in the forest?

TAKING CARE OF NATURE

Anytime we go into **nature**, we must take care of it. We should leave the forest as we found it.

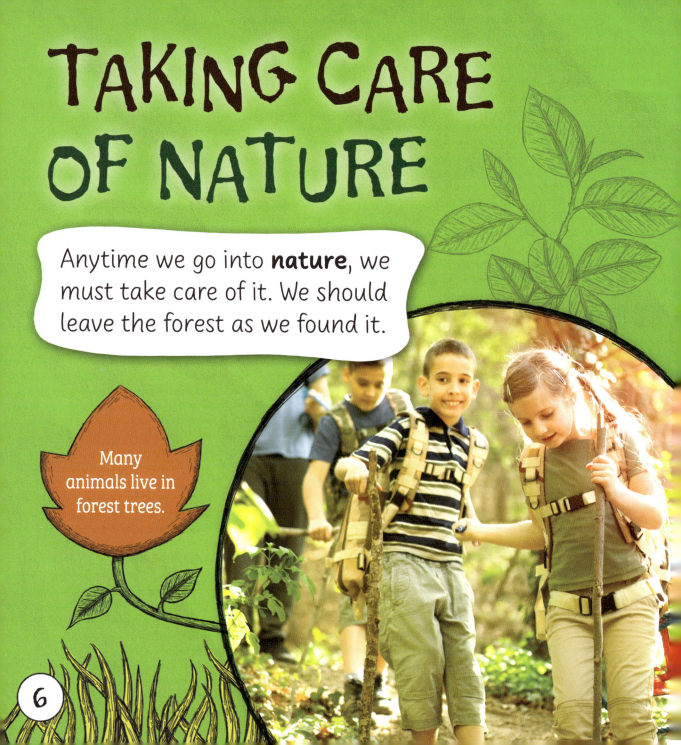

Many animals live in forest trees.

Stay on the path during forest school. That way, we won't hurt any animals or plants. What else can we do to care for the forest?

Let small trees and other plants grow instead of picking them.

It's okay to watch the animals that live near trees. But remember not to touch them.

Take away trash so it doesn't become **litter**.

INTO THE WOODS

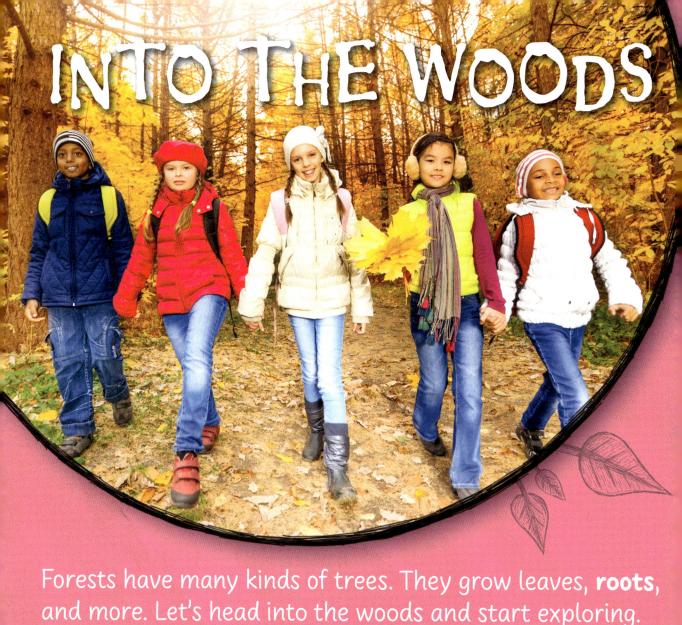

Forests have many kinds of trees. They grow leaves, **roots**, and more. Let's head into the woods and start exploring.

Leaves turn sunlight into food for trees. Roots soak up water from the ground. This food and water gives trees the **energy** they need to grow.

Have you seen different trees? What did they look like?

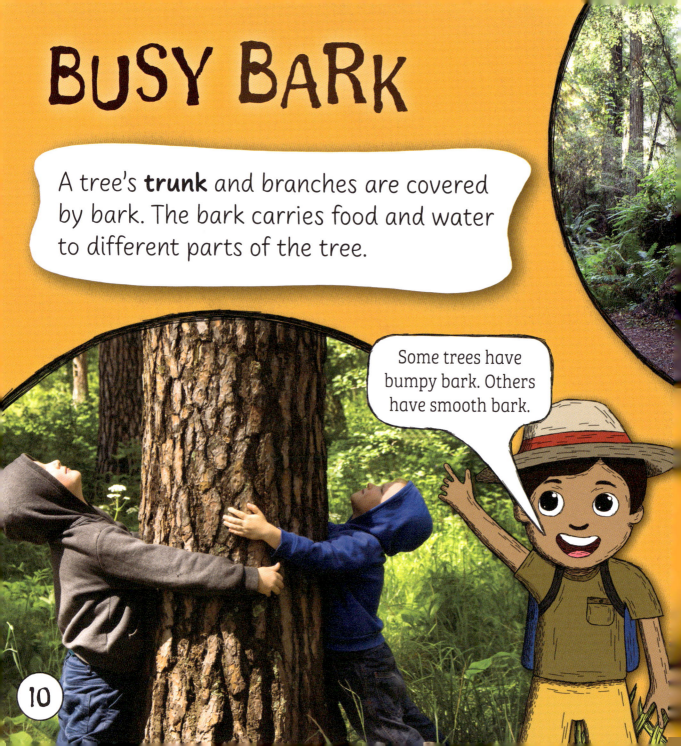

Tree trunk

Bark also **protects** the tree from wind, animals, and more. It is like the tree's skin.

Branches

Bugs can live in tree bark.

STICKS AND SEEDS

Most sticks you find on the ground were once tree branches. Birds use sticks to make nests. Bugs may use sticks for **shelter**, too.

Trees make seeds so new trees can grow. Even the tallest trees in the forest grew from small seeds.

Acorns make oak trees.

Horse chestnuts make horse chestnut trees.

These don't look alike, but they are all tree seeds!

Pinecones make pine trees.

FRUIT AND NUTS

Fruits have seeds in them. Apple trees grow fruit in forests.

Some animals eat seeds from trees.

CHANGING COLORS

In the fall, there is less daylight. The days get colder. This makes many tree leaves change color.

After leaves change color, they usually fall to the ground.

Pine trees have thin, pointy leaves. They are called needles. Needles stay green all year.

NEW GROWTH

After a tree's leaves fall, its branches are bare all winter. Then, in the spring, new leaves grow.

As a tree grows each year, its trunk gets wider. **Rings** inside the trunk show how old the tree is. A new ring grows each year.

Tree rings

Some trees grow flowers in the spring.

GET MAKING!

Have forest trees sparked your **creativity**? Let's try making something in nature.

Do you like colorful fall leaves? Gather some leaves from the ground. Then, glue them together to make a crown.

TIME TO THINK

Our time at forest school is almost over. Let's think about what we've learned.

Nature can be a great place to go and think.

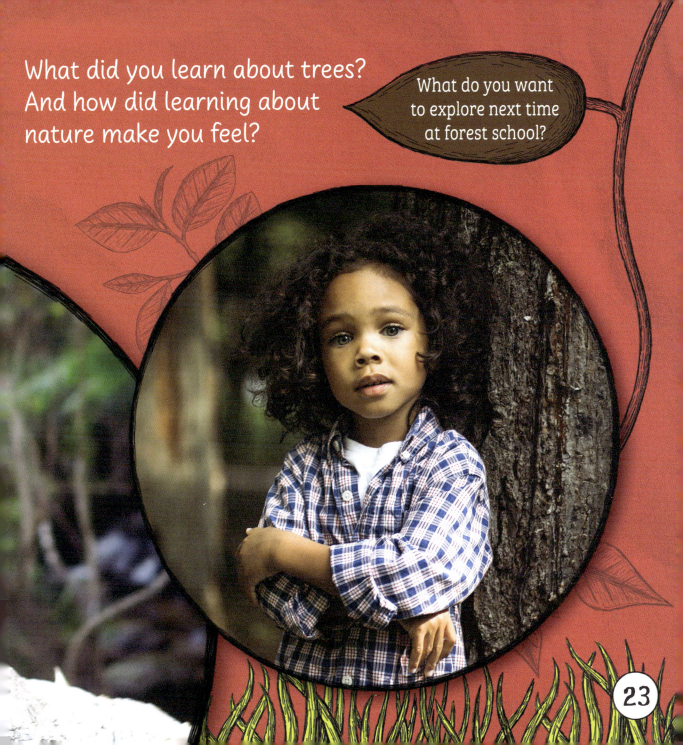
What did you learn about trees? And how did learning about nature make you feel?

What do you want to explore next time at forest school?

GLOSSARY

creativity the ability to imagine, make new things, or think new thoughts

energy power that can be used to do or make something

litter things that have been thrown on the ground

nature the world and everything in it that is not made by people

protects keeps something safe

rings round shapes that may go around something

roots the parts of a plant that grow underground

shelter a safe place to live

trunk the center part of a tree from which branches and roots grow

INDEX

bark 10–11
birds 12
bugs 11–12
colors 16, 20
fall 16, 18, 20
fruits 14–15
leaves 8–9, 16–18, 20
seeds 12–14
shelter 12
spring 18–19
sticks 12, 21